Selected Poems

Essential Poets Series 73

Émile Nelligan

Selected Poems

Bilingual Edition

*Translated from the French
by P. F. Widdows*

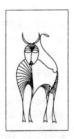

Guernica
Toronto / New York
1995

Selected Poems was originally published by Ryerson Press in 1960.

Antonio D'Alfonso, editor
Guernica Editions Inc.
P.O. Box 117, Station P, Toronto (Ontario), Canada M5S 2S6
340 Nagel Drive, Cheektowaga, N.Y. 14225-4731 U.S.A.

Typesetting by Jean Yves Collette.
Printed in Canada.

Legal Deposit – Third Quarter
National Library of Canada.

Library of Congress Catalog Card Number: 94-79586

Canadian Cataloguing in Publication Data

Nelligan, Émile, 1879-1941
[Poems. English & French. Selections]
Selected poems

(Essential Poets ; 73)
Poems in the original French with English translation.
Original publ. : Toronto : Ryerson Press. 1962
ISBN 0-55071-034-6

1 . Nelligan, Émile, 1879-1941 – Translations into English.
I . Widdows, p. f. (Paul Frederick), 1918-   .
II . Title.   III . Series.
PS8477 . E4A613 1995   C841 ' .54   C94-900783-B
PR9199 . 2 N45A613 1995

Table of Contents

6

Preface

Nelligan published his first poems, pseudony-
mously, in the Montreal newspaper *Le Samedi*.
In January, 1897, after a disastrous failure in the first
term's examinations, he left school with only one idea
in mind, to be a poet. Naturally such an ambition did
not appeal to his father, who made various attempts to
put him to work. In June, 1898, he travelled, appar-
ently as a sailor, to Liverpool, and two months later
was back in Montreal, the richer by a stock of marine
imagery if by nothing else. A job was found for him as
a clerk, and he left it after a week. After that his father
seems to have given up. At any rate he never again
submitted himself to what the world and his father
called work.

Work of his own kind, however, he had been
continuously and successfully doing ever since he had
left school, and if he did not gain wide public recogni-
tion, at least in his own circle he was admired and
valued. In the winter of 1896-1897 he had had the
good fortune to meet the man to whom more than to
anyone else is due the appreciation and publication of
his poetry, père Eugène Seers, known to literature by
his pseudonym of Louis Dantin. This strange and self-

tormented man, later to be an exile in Boston from his country and his Church, was widely travelled, widely read in poetry and a perceptive critic – exactly the broadening influence that Nelligan needed. Having discovered what he was convinced was a trace of genius in Nelligan, he encouraged and criticized his work, printed some of his religious poems in the magazine of his Order and later, after Nelligan's mental breakdown, prepared his collected poems for publication.

Earlier in the same year, 1897, just before leaving school, Nelligan had been introduced by another friend, the poet Arthur de Bussières, to *l'École littéraire de Montréal.* This 'school,' founded in 1895, was an association of young intellectuals and poets who met to read and discuss each other's work, and also the work of the new poets in France, the Parnassians and the Symbolists. The heyday of *l'École littéraire* corresponded with Nelligan's brief and erratic membership of it. It gave him exactly what he wanted. It was an *avant-garde* and rebellious movement which swept away the old tradition of French-Canadian poetry with its rhetorical poems on the Niagara Falls and the Death of Montcalm, and substituted as models Verlaine and Baudelaire – heady wine to anyone, to Nelligan intoxicating. Whether or not his actual introduction to these poets was due to *l'École Littéraire* is open to doubt. Independently he was remarkably well read in French poetry, within certain cleverly calculated limits. Louis Dantin gives his literary ancestors as, among others, Rimbaud, Verlaine and Rodenbach. Jean

Charbonneau, author of *l'École littéraire de Montréal*, cites his interest in Rimbaud, Leconte de Lisle, Baudelaire, Verlaine, Rodenbach and Rollinat. Albert Laberge, in *Peintres et écrivains d'hier et d'aujourd'hui*, tells us that he usually had in his pocket a volume of Stuart Merrill, Vielé-Griffin or Rodenbach. And Paul Wyczynski of the University of Ottawa has discovered a whole mass of illuminating echoes of poets whom he read either in volume form or in the contemporary Montreal press.

All these literary ancestors prompt a discussion of the degree of Nelligan's originality. It is sometimes said that his poems are little more than pastiches of his favourite writers, and particularly of Verlaine and Rodenbach. Certainly he is not original in the sense that Rimbaud is original. He did not create a new language of poetry. But our ideas of what constitutes originality have been considerably modified in recent years. Research into the sources of, for example, Coleridge and Keats has shown far more obligation to other writers, on the conscious or unconscious level, than was usually suspected, and it has not lessened the value of these poets. The poet has an unusually comprehensive and retentive memory – the Muses were the daughters of Mnemosyne. His originality consists not in what he uses, but in how he uses it. If he allows himself to be dominated by what he remembers, he is imitative. If he uses what he remembers for his own purposes, absorbing, reshaping and transforming it (as Coleridge transformed his travel books into 'The

Ancient Mariner'), the process can be a source of strength and enrichment. There are plenty of examples in Nelligan's poetry of excessive domination by his models. He had, after all, to serve his apprenticeship. 'Berceuse' is such an example, I think the only one in the following selection. Slight though it is, I have included this piece of homage to Verlaine for the musical skill of its handling. For the other poems here selected I would claim that they are, in the true sense of the word, original; that no one else could have written them; that when, by their themes or their cadences, they suggest their forerunners, they do so only in a superficial sense; and that Nelligan created his own synthesis of thought, sensation and words, his own poetic voice.

His range is admittedly a narrow one. His two principal themes are Regret, chiefly for the lost paradise of childhood, and the Ideal, the positive side of Regret. Subordinate to these are *Le Rêve,* a conception which is not clearly defined but which represents an escape from the disappointment of life, and *La Névrose,* again a nebulous but nevertheless an eloquent word for the anguish which resulted from the inadequacy of *Le Rêve* as a philosophy of life. Today he would perhaps have called it *Angst* or *La Nausée.* He is an almost entirely introspective poet. His rare outward-looking poems are not as successful as those in which he expresses, and thereby calms, his emotional torments. The only specimens of the objective type in this selection are 'Le Perroquet,' 'L'Idiote aux cloches,' and 'Le

Fou.' His central theme of regret for lost childhood is not unique to him, but I do not know of any more immediate and passionate expression of it than his.

Passionate feeling, of course, is not enough to make a poet. The poet works with words. And with words Nelligan was well equipped. He has been compared, like all poets who started young and finished early, with Rimbaud. In general the comparison is absurd, but they did have this in common, that they both came to their tasks fully armed. Nelligan found the images and symbols to express his feelings and embodied them with unerring tact in the appropriate words, rhythms and rhymes. There is no sense of straining after effect. One has the impression of a technique waiting to translate the ideas without distortion into the language of art. This does not mean that he achieved his effects without working for them. The interested reader will find a good example of his sure feeling for words in a comparison between the earlier and later versions of 'Soirs d'automne,' where all the changes made are for the better.

It has often been remarked that his verse moves with a natural music. That is true, as can be seen conspicuously in 'Rêve d'artiste,' 'Clair de lune intellectuel,' 'Le Jardin d'antan,' and 'Sérénade triste.' He was also, as is not so often recognized, capable of writing poems of great force and power, for example 'Le Vaisseau d'or,' 'Châteaux en Espagne,' and 'La Vierge noire'; and capable of combining the two effects in an harmonious whole, as in 'Ruines,' 'Amour immaculé' and 'Devant le feu.' He is also a poet of ressounding and memorable lines; and memorableness is an important test of a poet. One does not forget such lines as these:

> Or, depuis je me sens muré contre le monde
> Tel un prince du Nord que son Kremlin défend.

> Ma jeunesse qui va, comme un soldat passant,
> Au champ noir de la vie, arme au poing, tout en sang !

> Où son hymen chanta comme un rose poème.

> La fuite de l'Enfance au vaisseau des Vingt ans.

> Puisque, sous les outils des noirs maçons du Deuil,
> S'écroulent nos bonheurs comme des murs de briques.

> Tous ces oiseaux de bronze envolés des chapelles !

> Et j'entendais en moi des marteaux convulsifs
> Renfoncer les clous noirs des intimes Calvaires !

During the last year of his poetic career, 1899, Nelligan experienced a sense of mounting tension between himself as an artist and the uncomprehending society in which he lived. He had already had premonitions of disaster, had even said to Louis Dantin, 'Je mourrai fou – comme Baudelaire.' The occasion which led to his eventual collapse was in itself rather trivial. A visiting French journalist, E. de Marchy, made some adverse criticism of his poem 'Le Perroquet' at a meeting of *l'École littéraire*. Nelligan took this criticism very hard; took it, it seems, as an epitome of the brute world's opposition to the poet. Some two months later, on May 26, at a public meeting of *l'École littéraire* Nelligan read 'La Romance du vin,' his answer to de Marchy, his manifesto. Louis Dantin was present and has described the scene: 'When, with eyes blazing and with gestures exaggerated by his inner excitement, he declaimed his "Romance du vin" in passionate tones, a genuine thrill of emotion gripped the hall, and the applause took on the frenzy of an ovation.' Afterwards his colleagues carried him home on their shoulders.

It was his last appearance at *l'École littéraire.* His reason began to fail. He wandered about reciting scraps of poetry: he passed sleepless nights, or nights haunted by sinister dreams which he wrote down as poems the next day. ('Vision' is from this period). Finally on August 9 his parents took him to *la retraite Saint-Benoît,* suffering from a nervous disorder which was later described, on his transfer in 1925 to *l'hôpital Saint-Jean-de-Dieu,* as *dementia praecox.* He lived from 1899 until his death in 1941 in a state of remote indifference. Visits of friendship and of homage were paid to him, but he could only concentrate for short periods. Correctly had Louis Dantin opened his essay on Nelligan in 1902 with the words 'Émile Nelligan est mort.' The prophecy of 'Le Vaisseau d'or' had been true.

P. F. Widdows

For further information the reader is referred to two editions of Nelligan's poetry, both with long biographical and critical introductions in French:

Émile Nelligan et son œuvre, by Louis Dantin. Montreal, 1904. (reprinted in 1925, 1932 and 1945).

Émile Nelligan: *Poésies complètes, 1896-1899.* Edited and annotated by Luc Lacourcière. Éditions Fidès, Montreal 1952. 2nd Edition, 1958.

Also recommanded:

Émile Nelligan : sources et originalité de son œuvre, by Paul Wyczynski. Éditions de l'Université d'Ottawa, 1960.

Selected Poems

Clair de lune intellectuel

Ma pensée est couleur de lumières lointaines,
Du fond de quelque crypte aux vagues profondeurs.
Elle a l'éclat parfois des subtiles verdeurs
D'un golfe où le soleil abaisse ses antennes.

En un jardin sonore, au soupir des fontaines,
Elle a vécu dans les soirs doux, dans les odeurs ;
Ma pensée est couleur de lumières lointaines,
Du fond de quelque crypte aux vagues profondeurs.

Elle court à jamais les blanches prétentaines,
Au pays angélique où montent ses ardeurs,
Et, loin de la matière et des brutes laideurs,
Elle rêve l'essor aux célestes Athènes.

Ma pensée est couleur de lunes d'or lointaines.

The Mind's Moonlight

My thought is the colour of lights seen far away,
Deep in a crypt's mysterious emptiness.
Sometimes it shines with green's elusiveness
When the sun drops its shafts onto a bay.

In murmuring gardens, where the fountains play,
It has dwelt in the scents, in night's caress;
My thought is the colour of lights seen far away,
Deep in a crypt's mysterious emptiness.

Down the white thoroughfares it loves to stray
And climbs towards the land of happiness.
And, far from matter and brute ugliness,
It soars in dreams to Athens' brilliant day.

My thought is the colour of gold moons far away.

Le Vaisseau d'or

Ce fut un grand Vaisseau taillé dans l'or massif :
Ses mâts touchaient l'azur, sur des mers inconnues ;
La Cyprine d'amour, cheveux épars, chairs nues,
S'étalait à sa proue, au soleil excessif.

Mais il vint une nuit frapper le grand écueil
Dans l'Océan trompeur où chantait la Sirène,
Et le naufrage horrible inclina sa carène
Aux profondeurs du Gouffre, immuable cercueil.

Ce fut un Vaisseau d'Or, dont les flancs diaphanes
Révélaient des trésors que les marins profanes,
Dégoût, Haine et Névrose, entre eux ont disputés.

Que reste-t-il de lui dans la tempête brève ?
Qu'est devenu mon cœur, navire déserté ?
Hélas ! Il a sombré dans l'abîme du Rêve !

The Golden Ship

There was a fine Ship, carved from solid gold,
With azure-reaching masts, on seas unknown.
Spreadeagled Venus, naked, hair back-thrown,
Stood at the prow. The sun blazed uncontrolled.

But on the treacherous Ocean in the gloom
She struck the great reef where the Sirens chant.
Appalling shipwreck plunged her keel aslant
To the Gulf's depths, that unrelenting tomb.

She was a Golden Ship: but there showed through
Translucent sides treasures the blasphemous crew,
Hatred, Disgust and Madness, fought to share.

How much survives after the storm's brief race?
Where is my heart, that empty ship, oh where?
Alas, in Dream's abyss sunk without trace.

Clavier d'antan

Clavier vibrant de remembrance,
J'évoque un peu des jours anciens,
Et l'Éden d'or de mon enfance

Se dresse avec les printemps siens,
Souriant de vierge espérance
Et de rêves musiciens...

Vous êtes morte tristement,
Ma muse des choses dorées,
Et c'est de vous qu'est mon tourment ;

Et c'est pour vous que sont pleurées
Au luth âpre de votre amant
Tant de musiques éplorées.

Keyboard of the Past

A sounding-board of memories,
I summon up the long-ago
And see my childhood's Eden rise

Golden with Springs it used to know,
A-smile with lilting reveries
And virgin hopes. But now...

Now you are dead, my lost desire,
My muse of all the golden things;
It is from you, this torturing fire;

For your there rises from the strings
Of your fond lover's bitter lyre
The symphony of sorrowings.

Berceuse

Quelqu'un pleure dans le silence
Morne des nuits d'avril ;
Quelqu'un pleure la somnolence
Longue de son exil.
Quelqu'un pleure sa douleur
Et c'est mon cœur...

Lullaby

Someone weeps
In the April night's
Sad quietude;
Someone weeps
For his exiled life's
Long lassitude.
Someone weeps
For his sorrow's smart;
My heart it is, my heart...

Le Regret des joujoux

Toujours je garde en moi la tristesse profonde
Qu'y grava l'amitié d'une adorable enfant,
Pour qui la mort sonna le fatal olifant,
Parce qu'elle était belle et gracieuse et blonde.

Or, depuis je me sens muré contre le monde,
Tel un prince du Nord que son Kremlin défend,
Et, navré du regret dont je suis étouffant,
L'Amour comme à sept ans ne verse plus son onde.

Où donc a fui le jour des joujoux enfantins,
Lorsque Lucile et moi nous jouions aux pantins
Et courions tous les deux dans nos robes fripées ?

La petite est montée au fond des cieux latents,
Et j'ai perdu l'orgueil d'habiller ses poupées...
Ah ! de franchir si tôt le portail des vingt ans !

Nostalgia for Toys

My heart still holds the sorrow graven there
By love of a delightful child for whom
Death blew the summons on his horn of doom
For being beautiful and sweet and fair.

Since then, I feel walled in against the world,
A Kremlin-guarded ruler of the North,
And, stricken by my grief, from that year forth,
That seventh year, Love has his stream withheld.

The day of children's toys – Lucile and I
Playing with puppets, running side by side
In crumpled dresses – where is that lost day?

The little girl has climbed the distant sky,
And I no longer dress her dolls with pride...
So soon to pass my twentieth year's gateway!

Devant le feu

Par les hivers anciens quand nous portions la robe,
Tout petits, frais, rosés, tapageurs et joufflus,
Avec nos grands albums, hélas ! que l'on n'a plus,
Comme on croyait déjà posséder tout le globe !

Assis en rond, le soir, au coin du feu, par groupes,
Image sur image, ainsi combien joyeux
Nous feuilletions, voyant, la gloire dans les yeux,
Passer de beaux dragons qui chevauchaient en troupes !

Je fus de ces heureux d'alors, mais aujourd'hui,
Les pieds sur les chenets, le front terne d'ennui,
Moi qui me sens toujours l'amertume dans l'âme,

J'aperçois défiler, dans un album de flamme,
Ma jeunesse qui va, comme un soldat passant,
Au champ noir de la vie, arme au poing, toute en sang !

By the Fireside

In the old winters when we still were small,
In dresses, boisterous, pink, with chubby looks,
Our big and long-since vanished picture-books
Showed us the world; we seemed to own it all.

In groups around the fire at evening,
Picture by picture, ah! how happily
We turned the pages, starry-eyed to see
Squadrons of fine dragoons go galloping!

I once was happy, one of these; but now,
Feet on the fender, with dull, listless brown,
I with my always bitter heart descry

Flame-fashioned pictures where my youth goes by,
And, like a passing soldier, rides abroad
One life's black field, gripping a bloody sword.

Premier remords

Au temps où je portais des habits de velours,
Éparses sur mon col roulaient mes boucles brunes.
J'avais de grands yeux purs comme le clair des lunes ;
Dès l'aube je partais, sac au dos, les pas lourds.

Mais en route aussitôt je tramais des détours,
Et, narguant les pions de mes jeunes rancunes,
Je montais à l'assaut des pommes et des prunes
Dans les vergers bordant les murailles des cours.

Étant ainsi resté loin des autres élèves,
Loin des bancs, tout un mois, à vivre au gré des rêves,
Un soir, à la maison, craintif, comme j'entrais,

Devant le crucifix où sa lèvre se colle
Ma mère était en pleurs ! ... Ô mes ardents regrets !
Depuis, je fus toujours le premier à l'école.

First Remorse

In days before my velvet suits were shed,
My hair fell on my collar, curly brown.
Wide eyes I had, and pure, pure as the moon;
At dawn I left for school with feet of lead.

No sooner off, I planned détours instead.
I climbed to capture plums and apples grown
In orchards by the schoolyard, calling down
My young resentments on the teachers' heads.

A whole month I played truant, out of sight
Of boys and benches, dreaming, till one night,
When I crept guiltily into the house,

Mother was crying with her lips upon
The crucifix! And oh, my fierce remorse!
I was the first at school from that day on.

Ma mère

Quelquefois sur ma tête elle met ses mains pures,
Blanches, ainsi que des frissons blancs de guipures.

Elle me baise au front, me parle tendrement,
D'une voix au son d'or mélancoliquement.

Elle a les yeux couleur de ma vague chimère,
Ô toute poésie, ô toute extase, ô Mère !

À l'autel de ses pieds je l'honore en pleurant,
Je suis toujours petit pour elle, quoique grand.

My Mother

Sometimes upon my head she lays her hands, as chaste,
As white as are the soft ripples of snowy lace.

Her lips will touch my brow, and on my hearing fall
Her golden tones of voice, tender and sorrowful.

Her eyes are the faint shade of my perplexed desire,
O Mother, O all rapture, poetry entire!

Worshipping at her feet, I honour her with tears;
To her I still remain a child, despite the years.

Devant deux portraits de ma mère

Ma mère, que je l'aime en ce portrait ancien,
Peint aux jours glorieux qu'elle était jeune fille,
Le front couleur de lys et le regard qui brille
Comme un éblouissant miroir vénitien !

Ma mère que voici n'est plus du tout la même ;
Les rides ont creusé le beau marbre frontal ;
Elle a perdu l'éclat du temps sentimental
Où son hymen chanta comme un rose poème.

Aujourd'hui je compare, et j'en suis triste aussi,
Ce front nimbé de joie et ce front de souci,
Soleil d'or, brouillard dense au couchant des années.

Mais, mystère de cœur qui ne peut s'éclairer !
Comment puis-je sourire à ces lèvres fanées ?
Au portrait qui sourit, comment puis-je pleurer ?

CARL KOCH

SØREN KIERKEGAARD

ÉDITIONS "JE SERS" PARIS

Before Two Portraits of My Mother

I love my mother's portrait as she once
Was painted in her girlhood's glorious prime:
The forehead lily-white, the eyes that shine
With a Venetian mirror's brilliance!

Her other picture is a world away;
Wrinkles have ploughed the marble of her brow:
Lost is romance's rapture, distant now
The rose-red poem of her wedding day.

It saddens me today as I compare;
This brow haloed with joy, and that with care;
Gold sun, and thick mist at the years' eclipse.

But, O unfathomed mystery of the heart!
How can I smile at those poor faded lips?
How for the smiling face can teardrops start?

Le Jardin d'antan

Rien n'est plus doux aussi que de s'en revenir
        Comme après de longs ans d'absence,
                Que de s'en revenir
                Par le chemin du souvenir
                Fleuri de lys d'innocence,
                        Au jardin de l'Enfance.

Au jardin clos, scellé, dans le jardin muet
        D'où s'enfuirent les gaietés franches,
                Notre jardin muet
                Et la danse du menuet
                Qu'autrefois menaient sous branches
                        Nos sœurs en robes blanches.

Aux soirs d'avrils anciens, jetant des cris joyeux
        Entremêlés de ritournelles,
                Avec des *lieds* joyaux
                Elles passaient, la gloire aux yeux,
                Sous le frisson des tonnelles,
                        Comme en les villanelles

Cependant que venaient, du fond de la villa,
        Des accords de guitare ancienne,
                De la vieille villa,
                Et qui faisaient deviner là
                Près d'une obscure persienne,
                        Quelque musicienne.

The Garden of the Past

Nothing is sweeter than the glad return,
　　As after absent years abroad,
　　　　Sweeter than the return
　　　By memory's flower-bestrewn
　　　Lily-innocent road
　　　　To the garden of Childhood:

To the walled garden, private and entranced,
　　Where rang our fresh cries of delight,
　　　　Our walled garden entranced,
　　　Where once our sisters used to dance
　　　In the tree-dappled light,
　　　　Our sisters dressed in white.

On April evenings, with cries of joy,
　　Radiant, with refrains as well,
　　　　They passed with songs of joy
　　　Under the leafy canopy
　　　The arbour's sudden chill,
　　　　A living villanelle,

While somewhere from within the house came straying
　　An old guitar's accompaniment
　　　　From the old house came straying –
　　　Surely, you thought, a lady playing
　　　Behind cool shutters, bent
　　　　Over an instrument.

Mais rien n'est plus amer que de penser aussi
À tant de choses ruinées !
Ah ! de penser aussi,
Lorsque nous revenons ainsi
Par des sentes de fleurs fanées,
À nos jeunes années.

Lorsque nous nous sentons névrosés et vieillis,
Froissés, maltraités et sans armes,
Moroses et vieillis,
Et que, surnageant aux oublis,
S'éternise avec ses charmes
Notre jeunesse en larmes !

But what more bitter than to think also
      Of all those ruined things of ours!
         Alas! to think also
        When back across our lives we go
        By paths of withered flowers
          Back to our youthful years,

And feel ourselves neurotic, growing old,
      Ill-treated, slighted and disarmed,
         Surly and growing old;
        And struggling free from the lost world
        Our weeping youth becomes
          Eternal with its charms.

La Fuite de l'enfance

Par les jardins anciens foulant la paix des cistes
Nous revenons errer, comme deux spectres tristes,
Au seuil immaculé de la Villa d'antan.

Gagnons les bords fanés du Passé. Dans les râles
De sa joie il expire. Et vois comme pourtant
Il se dresse sublime en ses robes spectrales.

Ici sondons nos coeurs pavés de désespoirs.
Sous les arbres cambrant leurs massifs torses noirs
Nous avons les Regrets pour mystérieux hôtes.

Et bien loin, par les voies révolus et latents,
Suivons là-bas, devers les idéales côtes,
La fuite de l'Enfance au vaisseau des Vingt ans.

The Flight of Childhood

Trampling the wild-rose underfoot we come
Through the old gardens, back, like two sad ghosts,
To the pure threshold of our Villa home;

Come to the faded boundary of the lost
Past, which expires in throes of happiness.
Yet how majestic in its spectral dress!

Here let us plumb our hearts paved with despair.
We have Regrets mysteriously to share
The arching treetrunks' black immensity.

Far let us follow through the vanished night
To distant shores of innocence where, see,
Aboard my Twenty Years Childhood takes flight.

Ruines

Quelquefois je suis plein de grandes voix anciennes,
Et je revis un peu l'enfance en la villa ;
Je me retrouve encore avec ce qui fut là
Quand le soir nous jetait de l'or par les persiennes.

Et dans mon âme alors soudain je vois groupées
Mes sœurs à cheveux blonds jouant près des vieux feux ;
Autour d'elles le chat rôde, le dos frileux,
Les regardant vêtir, étonné, leurs poupées.

Ah ! la sérénité des jours à jamais beaux
Dont sont morts à jamais les radieux flambeaux,
Qui ne brilleront plus qu'en flammes chimériques :

Puisque tout est défunt, enclos dans le cercueil,
Puisque, sous les outils des noirs maçons du Deuil,
S'écroulent nos bonheurs comme des murs de briques !

Ruins

Sometimes I hear the voices heard of old,
And I relive my childhood, visiting
Awhile those villa days when evening
Aslant the shutters cast us down its gold.

And in my mind's eye suddenly I see
My fair-haired sisters playing by the hearth;
Round them the cat, spine bristling, picks his path,
Watching them dress their dolls, perplexedly.

Ah, the sweet calm! Forever splendid days!
Forever dead, their radiant flamboys,
Only with fancied flames henceforth to blaze:

For all is over, coffined; for beneath
The tools of the black stonemasons of Grief
Like walls of brick must crumble all our joys.

Les Angéliques

Des soirs, j'errais en lande hors du hameau natal,
Perdu parmi l'orgueil serein des grands monts roses,
Et les Anges, à flots de longs timbres moroses,
Ébranlaient les bourdons, au vent occidental.

Comme un berger-poète au cœur sentimental,
J'aspirais leur prière en l'arôme des roses,
Pendant qu'aux ors mourants, mes troupeaux de névroses
Vagabondaient le long des forêts de santal.

Ainsi, de par la vie où j'erre solitaire,
J'ai gardé dans mon âme un coin de vieille terre,
Paysage ébloui des soirs que je revois ;

Alors que, dans ta lande intime, tu rappelles,
Mon cœur, ces angélus d'antan, fanés, sans voix :
Tous ces oiseaux de bronze envolés des chapelles !

Evening Bells

Some evenings I roamed the moors, beyond the bounds
Of my home village, lost in the great rosy hills'
Calm pride, and down the wind the Angels shook the bells
Of churches in long waves of melancholy sound.

And in a shepherd-poet's dreamy, romantic mood
In the perfume of roses I used to breathe their prayer,
While in the dying gold my flocks of mania
Aimlessly wandered through forests of sandalwood.

Thus in this life where I follow my lonely path
I have kept in my mind a corner of old earth,
That evening countryside whose glow I see again;

While you, my heart, within your private reach of moor,
Recall the long-ago angelus, voiceless, faint:
That winging of bronze birds flown from the chapel towers.

Le Berceau de la muse

De mon berceau d'enfant j'ai fait l'autre berceau
Où ma Muse s'endort dans des trilles d'oiseau,
Ma Muse en robe blanche, ô ma toute maîtresse !

Oyez nos baisers d'or aux grands soirs familiers...
Mais chut ! j'entends déjà la mégère Détresse
À notre seuil faisant craquer ses noirs souliers !

The Muse's Cradle

From childhood's cradle I have shaped this other,
Where sleeps my Muse while birdsong trills above her,
My white-robed Muse, my one and only dear!

Those golden kisses at day's kindly close...
But hush! already at our door I hear
The harridan Distress creak her black shoes.

Rêve d'artiste

Parfois j'ai le désir d'une soeur bonne et tendre,
D'une sœur angélique au sourire discret :
Sœur qui m'enseignera doucement le secret
De prier comme il faut, d'espérer et d'attendre.

J'ai ce désir très pur d'une sœur éternelle,
D'une sœur d'amitié dans le règne de l'Art,
Qui me saura veillant à ma lampe très tard
Et qui me couvrira des cieux de sa prunelle ;

Qui me prendra les mains quelquefois dans les siennes
Et me chuchotera d'immaculés conseils,
Avec le charme ailé des voix musiciennes ;

Et pour qui je ferai, si j'aborde à la gloire,
Fleurir tout un jardin de lys et de soleils
Dans l'azur d'un poème offert à sa mémoire.

A Poet's Dream

Sometimes I crave a sister, sweet and good,
An angel-sister with a quiet smile:
One who will teach me in her gentle style
To hope, to wait and to pray as I should.

So pure a wish! A timeless sister-friend,
Companion in the realm of art, who'll wait
Beside me in the lamplight working late;
And on me like the sky her gaze she'll bend.

Sometimes she'll take my hands between her own
And whisper words of guidance, perfect ones,
All the winged charm of music in her tone.

And I shall bring to flower, If I find fame,
A garden full of lilies and of suns
In a bright azure poem to her name.

Amour immaculé

Je sais en une église un vitrail merveilleux
Où quelque artiste illustre, inspiré des archanges,
A peint d'une façon mystique, en robe à franges,
Le front nimbé d'un astre, une Sainte aux yeux bleus.

Le soir, l'esprit hanté de rêves nébuleux
Et du céleste écho de récitals étranges,
Je m'en viens la prier sous les lueurs oranges
De la lune qui luit entre ses blonds cheveux.

Telle sur le vitrail de mon cœur je t'ai peinte,
Ma romanesque aimée, ô pâle et blonde sainte,
Toi, la seule que j'aime et toujours aimerai ;

Mais tu restes muette, impassible, et, trop fière,
Tu te plais à me voir, sombre et désespéré,
Errer dans mon amour comme en un cimetière !

Stainless Love

There is a fine glass in a church I know
Where a great artist, by archangels blessed,
Has painted mystically, in a bordered dress,
A Saint with blue eyes and star-haloed brow.

When the celestial echoes of strange airs
At evening haunt my mind, and cloudy dreams,
I come to pray to her in the yellow beams
Of the moon shining through her golden hair.

So on my heart's glass window did I paint
You, my romantic love, O pale, fair saint,
Who are my one love, who will ever be;

But you stay silent, cool; too proud you are,
Happy to watch me, plunged in dark despair,
Roam round my love, as through a cemetery.

Châteaux en Espagne

Je rêve de marcher comme un conquistador,
Haussant mon labarum triomphal de victoire,
Plein de fierté farouche et de valeur notoire,
Vers des assauts de ville aux tours de bronze et d'or.

Comme un royal oiseau, vautour, aigle ou condor,
Je rêve de planer au divin territoire,
De brûler au soleil mes deux ailes de gloire
À vouloir dérober le céleste Trésor.

Je ne suis hospodar ni grand oiseau de proie ;
À peine si je puis dans mon cœur qui guerroie
Soutenir le combat des vieux Anges impurs ;

Et mes rêves altiers fondent comme des cierges
Devant cette Ilion éternelle aux cent murs,
La ville de l'Amour imprenable des Vierges !

Castles in Spain

Fierce in my pride, for bravery renowned,
In dreams I march like a conquistador,
Flying my conquering labarum before,
To storm the gold and bronze-embattled towns.

Like a royal bird, a vulture, eagle, condor,
I soar in dreams to the gods' territory
And scorch beneath the sun my two-winged glory,
Seeking the Treasure of the skies for plunder.

I am no hospodar, no great bird of prey,
Hard put to it in my warring heart to stay
The vicious Angels raging to destroy;

And my high dreams like waxen candles melt
Before this hundred-walled eternal Troy,
Love's city, impregnable, by Virgins held.

Soir d'hiver

Ah ! comme la neige a neigé !
Ma vitre est un jardin de givre.
Ah ! comme la neige a neigé !
Qu'est-ce que le spasme de vivre
À la douleur que j'ai, que j'ai !

Tous les étangs gisent gelés,
Mon âme est noire : Où vis-je ? Où vais-je ?
Tous ses espoirs gisent gelés :
Je suis la nouvelle Norvège
D'où les blonds ciels s'en sont allés.

Pleurez, oiseaux de février,
Au sinistre frisson des choses,
Pleurez, oiseaux de février,
Pleurez mes pleurs, pleurez mes roses,
Aux branches du génévrier.

Ah ! comme la neige a neigé !
Ma vitre est un jardin de givre.
Ah ! comme la neige a neigé !
Qu'est-ce que le spasme de vivre
À tout l'ennui que j'ai, que j'ai ! ...

Winter Evening

Ah! how the snow has snowed!
My glass is a garden of frost.
Ah! how the snow has snowed!
What is life's brief outburst
To the grief that I know, I know?

Now all the ponds lie frozen.
My soul is dark: where stay?
Where go? Its hopes lie frozen:
I am that new Norway
Whose pale blue skies have flown.

Weep, winter birds exposed
To the world's sinister shiver,
Weep, winter birds exposed;
To the boughs of the juniper
Weep for my tears, my roses.

Ah! how the snow has snowed!
My glass is a garden of frost.
Ah! how the snow has snowed!
What is life's brief outburst
To the dull void that I know?

Rondel à ma pipe

Les pieds sur les chenets de fer
Devant un bock, ma bonne pipe,
Selon notre amical principe
Rêvons à deux, ce soir d'hiver.

Puisque le ciel me prend en grippe
(N'ai-je pourtant assez souffert ?)
Les pieds sur les chenets de fer
Devant un bock, rêvons, ma pipe.

Preste, la mort que j'anticipe
Va me tirer de cet enfer
Pour celui du vieux Lucifer ;
Soit ! Nous fumerons chez ce type,

Les pieds sur les chenets de fer.

Roundel to My Pipe

Feet on the fender by firelight,
With glass in hand, good pipe, content,
Let's keep our friendly precedent
And dream alone, this winter night.

Since heaven has grown so virulent,
(As though my troubles were too slight!)
Feet on the fender by firelight,
With glass in hand, let's dream, content.

Soon death, by my presentiment,
Will drag me from this hellish site
To good old Lucifer's; all right!
We'll smoke in that establishment,

Feet on the fender by firelight.

Soirs d'automne

Voici que la tulipe et voilà que les roses,
Sous le geste massif des bronzes et des marbres,
Dans le Parc où l'Amour folâtre sous les arbres,
Chantent dans les longs soirs monotones et roses.

Dans les soirs a chanté la gaîté des parterres,
Où danse un clair de lune en des poses obliques,
Et de grands souffles vont, lourds et mélancoliques,
Troubler le rêve blanc des oiseaux solitaires.

Voici que la tulipe et voilà que les roses
Et les lys cristallins, pourprés de crépuscule,
Rayonnent tristement au soleil qui recule,
Emportant la douleur des bêtes et des choses.

Et mon amour meurtri, comme une chair qui saigne,
Repose sa blessure et calme ses névroses.
Et voici que les lys, la tulipe et les roses
Pleurent les souvenirs où mon âme se baigne.

Autumn Evenings

See here the tulip, and see there the roses,
Where in the Park Love sports beneath the trees,
Sing in the long rose-red, unruffled eves
Under the bronze and marble's massive poses.

Gaily at night have sung the flower-beds
On which the slanting moonbeams pirouette,
And gusts of wind blow heavy, desolate,
Troubling the white dream of the lonely birds.

See here the tulip, and see there the roses
And lilies dusk-empurpled, crystalline,
Gleam sadly in the sun that now declines;
And now the pain of things and creatures closes.

My shattered love is bruised and raw; but see,
The quivering nerves grow still, the hurt reposes.
And the lily now, the tulip and the roses
Watch my soul bathe in memories, and weep.

La Cloche dans la brume

Écoutez, écoutez, ô ma pauvre âme ! Il pleure
Tout au loin dans la brume ! Une cloche ! Des sons
Gémissent sous le noir des nocturnes frissons,
Pendant qu'une tristesse immense nous effleure.

À quoi songez-vous donc ? à quoi pensez vous tant ? ...
Vous qui ne priez plus, ah ! serait-ce, pauvresse,
Que vous compareriez soudain votre détresse
À la cloche qui rêve aux angélus d'antan ? ...

Comme elle vous geignez, funèbre et monotone,
Comme elle vous tintez dans les brouillards d'automne,
Plainte de quelque église exilée en la nuit,

Et qui regrette avec de sonores souffrances
Les fidèles quittant son enceinte qui luit,
Comme vous regrettez l'exil des Espérances.

The Bell in the Mist

Listen, my poor soul, listen! A sob, a sigh
Far off in the mist! A bell! A moaning quiver
Throbs underneath the dark of the night-shiver,
And we are touched by a vast melancholy.

What are the dreams, the thoughts that hold you fast?
You who no longer pray, ah! could it be
That your poor anguish matches suddenly
The bell which dreams of angeluses past?

Like it you keen on one grey note, my soul,
Like it across the autumn mist you toll
The dirge of a church exiled in the night,

Which plaintively laments the faithful group
Leaving its island sanctuary of light,
As you regret the exile of your Hopes.

Christ en croix

Je remarquais toujours ce grand Jésus de plâtre
Dressé comme un pardon au seuil du vieux couvent,
Échafaud solennel à geste noir, devant
Lequel je me courbais, saintement idolâtre.

Or, l'autre soir, à l'heure où le cri-cri folâtre,
Par les prés assombris, le regard bleu rêvant,
Récitant Eloa, les cheveux dans le vent,
Comme il sied à l'Éphèbe esthétique et bellâtre,

J'aperçus, adjoignant des débris de parois,
Un gigantesque amas de lourde vieille croix
Et de plâtre écroulé parmi les primevères ;

Et je restai là, morne, avec les yeux pensifs,
Et j'entendais en moi des marteaux convulsifs
Renfoncer les clous noirs des intimes Calvaires !

Christ on the Cross

This plaster Jesus always halted me,
Placed like a shrine at the old covent door,
A scaffold, stern and lowering, before
Which I would bend with meek idolatry.

Not long ago, in blue-eyed reverie
Roaming dim meadows at the cricket's hour
With wind-blown hair, declaiming 'Eloa',
True to my rôle of art's young devotee,

I noticed near the ruins of that wall
Piled high, the ancient, massive cross with all
The plaster crumbled in the primroses.

And I stayed staring, sad, contemplative,
And heard in me convulsive hammers drive
Home the black nails of private Calvaries.

Sérénade triste

Comme des larmes d'or qui de mon cœur s'égouttent,
Feuilles de mes bonheurs, vous tombez toutes, toutes.

Vous tombez au jardin de rêve où je m'en vais,
Où je vais, les cheveux au vent des jours mauvais.

Vous tombez de l'intime arbre blanc, abattues
Çà et là, n'importe où dans l'allée aux statues.

Couleurs des jours anciens, de mes robes d'enfant,
Quand les grands vents d'automne ont sonné l'olifant.

Et vous tombez toujours, mêlant vos agonies,
Vous tombez, mariant, pâles, vos harmonies.

Vous avez chu dans l'aube au sillon des chemins ;
Vous pleurez de mes yeux, vous tombez de mes mains.

Comme des larmes d'or qui de mon coeur s'égouttent,
Dans mes vingt ans déserts vous tombez toutes, toutes.

Lament

Like tears, like golden tears from my heart dropping down,
Leaves of my happiness, you fall each one, each one.

You fall in the dream garden where I go my way,
Go with my hair stirred by the wind of evil days.

You fall stricken beneath the intimate white tree,
Whirled down the statued walk, here, there, haphazardly;

Colour of childhood's dress, colour of days long gone
When the great autumn winds blew on their ivory horn.

And still you fall, you fall, blending your agonies,
You fall and interfuse, pallid, your harmonies.

You have come down at dawn onto the furrowed lanes,
You weep from my own eyes, you fall from my own hands.

Like tears, like golden tears from my heart dropping down,
On my twenty desert years you fall each one, each one.

Tristesse blanche

Et nos cœurs sont profonds et vides comme un gouffre,
Ma chère, allons-nous-en, tu souffres et je souffre.

Fuyons vers le castel de nos Idéals blancs
Oui, fuyons la Matière aux yeux ensorcelants.

Aux plages de Thulé, vers l'île des Mensonges,
Sur la nef des vingt ans fuyons comme des songes.

Il est un pays d'or plein de *lieds* et d'oiseaux,
Nous dormirons tous deux aux frais lits des roseaux,

Nous nous reposerons des intimes désastres,
Dans des rythmes de flûte, à la valse des astres.

Fuyons vers le château de nos Idéals blancs,
Oh ! fuyons la Matière aux yeux ensorcelants.

Veux-tu mourir, dis-moi ? Tu souffres et je souffre,
Et nos cœurs sont profonds et vides comme un gouffre.

Elegy in White

And our two hearts are deep and empty utterly;
My dear, let us depart, we suffer, you and I.

Let us flee to the keep that guards our white Ideals,
Yes, let us flee from Fact whose witching eyes compel.

To Thule's shores, towards the island of Illusion,
Aboard the ship of Twenty let us escape like visions.

There lies a golden land, song-haunted, full of birds;
And we will sleep together on the reeds' fragrant beds.

There we will find relief after the blows of fate
To the waltz of the stars, in rhythms of the flute.

Let us flee to the castle that guards our white Ideals,
Oh! let us flee from Fact whose witching eyes compel.

Are you prepared for death? We suffer, you and I,
And our two hearts are deep and empty utterly.

La Passante

Hier, j'ai vu passer, comme une ombre qu'on plaint,
En un grand parc obscur, une femme voilée :
Funèbre et singulière, elle s'en est allée,
Recélant sa fierté sous son masque opalin.

Et rien que d'un regard, par ce soir cristallin,
J'eus deviné bientôt sa douleur refoulée ;
Puis elle disparut en quelque noire allée
Propice au deuil profond dont son cœur était plein.

Ma jeunesse est pareille à la pauvre passante :
Beaucoup la croiseront ici-bas dans la sente
Où la vie à la tombe âprement nous conduit ;

Tous la verront passer, feuille sèche à la brise
Qui tourbillonne, tombe et se fane en la nuit ;
Mais nul ne l'aimera, nul ne l'aura comprise.

A Woman Passing By

A woman in a veil. In the darkening park
Ghostlike she passed before me yesterday.
Mournful and singular she moved away
Hiding her pride beneath an opal mask.

One look from her was all I had to ask
To guess the grief that secret in her lay.
And then she vanished down a shadowy way
That seemed to match her mourning, dark to dark.

Compare my youth to that poor passer-by.
Many will meet it here, where joylessly
Life leads us down the pathway to the tomb;

All see it pass, like a leaf in the wind
That twists and falls and withers in the gloom:
But none will love it, none will understand.

La Vierge noire

Elle a les yeux pareils à d'étranges flambeaux
Et ses cheveux d'or faux sur ses maigres épaules,
Dans des subtils frissons de feuillages de saules,
L'habillent comme font les cyprès des tombeaux.

Elle porte toujours ses robes par lambeaux,
Elle est noire et méchante ; or qu'on la mette aux geôles,
Qu'on la batte à jamais à grands fouets de tôles.
Gare d'elle, mortels, c'est la chair des corbeaux !

Elle m'avait souri d'une bonté profonde,
Je l'aurais crue aimable et sans souci du monde,
Nous nous serions tenus, Elle et moi, par les mains.

Mais, quand je lui parlai, le regard noir d'envie,
Elle me dit : tes pas ont souillé mes chemins.
Certes tu la connais, on l'appelle la Vie !

The Dark Maiden

Her eyes are like strange torches: golden hair,
Whose gold is counterfeit, falls down to dress
Thin shoulders with the subtle restlessness
Of willow leaves: so tombs their cypress wear.

Her gowns are always ragged, and her air
Is dark and evil: hold her in duress,
Lash her with rods of iron, merciless!
She is crows' carrion: mortals, beware!

With profound goodness she had smiled on me;
I would have thought her kind and fancy-free,
We would have held hands, She and I. Instead,

When I spoke out, dark longing in my eyes,
'Your steps have made my paths unclean,' she said.
Her name is Life: one you will recognize.

L'Idiote aux Cloches

I

Elle a voulu trouver les cloches
Du jeudi saint sur les chemins ;
Elle a saigné ses pieds aux roches
À les chercher dans les soirs maints,
        Ah ! lon lan laire,
Elle a meurtri ses pieds aux roches ;
On lui disait : « Fouille tes poches.
— Nenni, sont vers les cieux romains :
Je veux trouver les cloches, cloches,
        Je veux trouver les cloches
Et je les aurai dans mes mains » ;
Ah ! lon lan laire et lon lan la.

II

Or vers les heures vespérales
Elle allait, solitaire, aux bois.
Elle rêvait des cathédrales
Et des cloches dans les beffrois ;
        Ah ! lon lan laire,
Elle rêvait des cathédrales,
Puis tout à coup, en de fous râles
S'élevait tout au loin sa voix :
« Je veux trouver les cloches, cloches,
        Je veux trouver les cloches
Et je les aura dans mes mains » ;
Ah ! lon lan laire et lon lan la.

The Idiot Girl

I

The bells of Holy Week, she tried
To find them all along the roads;
On the sharp stones her poor feet bled
As on her evening quests she roamed,
　　Ah! fol derol day,
On the cruel stones her poor feet bled;
'Try in your pockets,' people cried
'No, no, nearer the skies of Rome:
I want to find the bells, the bells,
　　I want to find the bells,
And I will hold them in my hands':
Ah! fol derol lol derol day.

II

Then she would go among the shaws,
Alone she went at evening
She dreamed of the cathedral towers
And of the bells that in them ring;
　　Ah! fol derol day,
She dreamed of the cathedral towers,
Then suddenly, confused and hoarse
Her voice far off came clamouring:
'I want to find the bells, the bells,
　　I want to find the bells,
And I will hold them in my hands':
Ah! fol derol lol derol day.

Une aube triste, aux routes croches,
On la trouva dans un fossé.
Dans la nuit du retour des cloches
L'idiote avait trépassé ;
      Ah ! lon lan laire,
Dans la nuit du retour des cloches,
À leurs métalliques approches,
Son rêve d'or fut exaucé :
Un ange mit les cloches, cloches,
      Lui mit toutes les cloches,
Là-haut, lui mit toutes aux mains :
Ah ! lon lan laire et lon lan la.

III

By winding byways one sad dawn
They found her: in a ditch she lay.
On that night when the bells return
The idiot girl had passed away;
    Ah! fol derol day,
On that night when the bells return
Her golden dream came true, as on
And on the brazen clangour came:
An angel put the bells, the bells,
    On high put all the bells
Put all of them between her hands;
Ah! fol derol lol derol day.

Le Perroquet

Aux jours de sa vieille détresse
Elle avait, la pauvre négresse,
Gardé cet oiseau d'allégresse.

Ils habitaient, au coin hideux,
Un de ces réduits hasardeux,
Au faubourg lointain, tous les deux.

Lui, comme jadis à la foire,
Il jacassait les jours de gloire
Perché sur son épaule noire.

La vieille écoutait follement,
Croyant que par l'oiseau charmant
Causait l'âme de son amant.

Car le poète chimérique,
Avec une verve ironique
À la crédule enfant d'Afrique

Avait conté qu'il s'en irait,
À son trépas, vivre en secret
Chez l'âme de son perroquet.

C'est pourquoi la vieille au front chauve,
À l'heure où la clarté se sauve,
Interrogeait l'oiseau, l'œil fauve.

The Parrot

In her last days the poor negress
Had kept, through old age and distress,
This bird with its gay jauntiness.

They lived down on a hideous back
Street in a rickety old shack,
Together, out beyond the tracks.

On her black shoulder it would shrill
Away in its old fair-time style
Of the great days remembered still.

The old dame trembled at the words,
Thinking that through the pretty bird
It was her lover's soul she heard.

He was a poet, with a veiled
Ironic wit, and had beguiled
Africa's over-credulous child:

Into her parrot's soul, when dead,
He would be safely spirited
And lodge there secretly, he said.

And so the old bald-headed thing
In the last light of evening
Would start her wild-eyed questioning.

Mais lui riait, criant toujours,
Du matin au soir tous les jours :
« Ha ! Ha ! Ha ! Gula, mes amours ! »

Elle en mourut dans un cri rauque,
Croyant que sous le soliloque
Inconscient du bavard glauque,

L'amant défunt voulait, moqueur,
Railler l'amour de son vieux cœur.
Elle en mourut dans la rancœur.

L'oiseau pleura ses funérailles,
Puis se fit un nid de pierrailles
En des ruines de murailles.

Mais il devint comme hanté ;
Et quand la nuit avait chanté
Au clair du ciel diamanté,

On eût dit, à voir sa détresse,
Qu'en lui pleurait, dans sa tendresse,
L'âme de la pauvre négresse.

The bird laughed, screeching all the time,
From morn till eve, all the long time,
'Ha! Ha! Gula, those loves of mine!'

She died of it, in a hoarse scream,
Thinking that underneath the stream
Of the glib, mindless chatterer's theme

The dead man used this mocking art
To taunt the love of her old heart:
She died of it, the bitter hurt.

The bird wept at her funeral,
Then built itself a ramshackle
Stone nest among a ruined wall,

And became haunted, seemingly;
For when night sang her melody
Illumined by the spangled sky

One would have said, seeing its distress,
The spirit of the poor negress
Wept in the bird, all tenderness.

La Romance du vin

Tout se mêle en un vif éclat de gaîté verte.
Ô le beau soir de mai ! Tous les oiseaux en chœur,
Ainsi que les espoirs naguères à mon cœur,
Modulent leur prélude à ma croisée ouverte.

Ô le beau soir de mai ! le joyeux soir de mai !
Un orgue au loin éclate en froides mélopées ;
Et les rayons, ainsi que de pourpres épées,
Percent le cœur du jour qui se meurt parfumé.

Je suis gai ! je suis gai ! Dans le cristal qui chante,
Verse, verse le vin ! verse encore et toujours,
Que je puisse oublier la tristesse des jours,
Dans le dédain que j'ai de la foule méchante !

Je suis gai ! je suis gai ! Vive le vin et l'Art ! ...
J'ai le rêve de faire aussi des vers célèbres,
Des vers qui gémiront les musiques funèbres
Des vents d'automne au loin passant dans le brouillard.

C'est le règne du rire amer et de la rage
De se savoir poète et l'objet du mépris,
De se savoir un cœur et de n'être compris
Que par le clair de lune et les grands soirs d'orage !

Femmes ! je bois à vous qui riez du chemin
Où l'Idéal m'appelle en ouvrant ses bras roses ;
Je bois à vous surtout, hommes aux fronts moroses
Qui dédaignez ma vie et repoussez ma main !

The Poet's Wine

The fine May evening is interfused
With a bright glow of verdant gaiety.
Birds at my window trill their melody
And hope sings in my heart, as once it used.

O fine, O joyous evening of May!
A distant organ throbs its frigid chords;
And the long sunbeam-shafts, like purple swords
Pierce to the heart the sweetly-dying day.

How gay, how gay am I! Fill, fill the glass,
The singing glass – again, and yet again,
That I may spurn the evil throng of men
And so forget how sad my days do pass.

How gay am I! To wine and Art, all praise!
I dream of making poems that will find
Renown, and sigh the haunting dirge of winds
Moving in autumn through the distant haze.

Today, the bitter laugh, the rage; to sense
The poet's certainty of power and stand
Despised; to be a heart none understands
But moonlight and the night storm's violence.

Women! I drink to you who mock the way
The open-armed Ideal calls me to:
And, surly bores, a special toast to you
Who scorn my life and thrust my hand away.

Pendant que tout l'azur s'étoile dans la gloire,
Et qu'un hymne s'entonne au renouveau doré,
Sur le jour expirant je n'ai pas donc pleuré,
Moi qui marche à tâtons dans ma jeunesse noire !

Je suis gai ! je suis gai ! Vive le soir de mai !
Je suis follement gai, sans être pourtant ivre ! ...
Serait-ce que je suis enfin heureux de vivre ;
Enfin mon cœur est-il guéri d'avoir aimé ?

Les cloches ont chanté ; le vent du soir odore...
Et pendant que le vin ruisselle à joyeux flots,
Je suis si gai, si gai, dans mon rire sonore,
Oh ! si gai, que j'ai peur d'éclater en sanglots !

While the star-vault in glory pricks alight
And a hymn swells to praise the gilded spring,
I have not wept at day's extinguishing,
I who am groping through my youth's dark night.

May evening! How gay, how gay am I!
Wild gaiety, and yet no drunkenness.
Can I at last greet life with happiness?
Is my heart healed of love's long malady?

The clocks have chimed: the fragrant breezes make
The evening sweet, and while the wine flows free
So gay am I, in laughing revelry,
So gay that oh, I fear my heart will break!

Vision

Or, j'ai la vision d'ombres sanguinolentes
    Et de chevaux fougueux piaffants,
Et c'est comme des cris de gueux, hoquets d'enfants,
    Râles d'expirations lentes.

D'où me viennent, dis-moi, tous les ouragans rauques,
    Rages de fifre ou de tambour ?
On dirait des dragons en galopade au bourg,
    Avec des casques flambant glauques...

FRAGMENT III

Le Fou

Gondolar ! Gondolar !
Tu n'es plus sur le chemin très tard.

On assassina l'pauvre idiot,
On l'écrasa sous un chariot,
Et puis l'chien après l'idiot.

On leur fit un grand, grand trou là.
    Dies irae, dies illa
À genoux devant ce trou-là !

Vision

Nightmare of shadows bloody-red,
Fierce prancing horses, and what seems
Beggars' shrill whining, children's screams,
Death-rattles slowly, slowly dead.

From where these hurricanes roaring down,
Thunderous alarm of fife or drum?
Are these dragoons? Full gallop they come –
Dull glint of helmets through a town...

FRAGMENT III

The Madman

Gondolar! Gondolar!
You're out late on the road no more.

They murdered the poor idiot,
They crushed him underneath a cart,
And his dog after the idiot.

They dug them a big, big hole, they did.
    Dies irae, dies illa
Down on your knees in front of it.

Je sens voler

Je sens voler en moi les oiseaux du génie
Mais j'ai tendu si mal mon piège qu'ils ont pris
Dans l'azur cérébral leurs vols blancs, bruns et gris,
Et que mon cœur brisé râle son agonie.

I Feel the Birds of Genius

I feel the birds of genius flying in me,
But I prepared my trap so clumsily
That they have taken their white,
Their brown and their grey flight
Into the spirit's azure, leaving me
My stricken heart strangling in agony.

Printed in November 1995 by

VEILLEUX
IMPRESSION À DEMANDE INC.

in Boucherville, Quebec